Whisked Away

Poems for more than one voice

Richard Brown

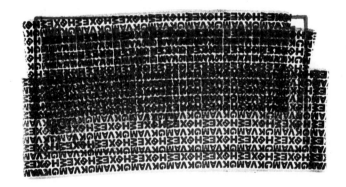

CAMBRIDGE
UNIVERSITY PRESS

Published by the Press Syndicate of the University of Cambridge
The Pitt Building, Trumpington Street, Cambridge CB2 1RP
40 West 20th Street, New York, NY 10011–4211, USA
10 Stamford Road, Oakleigh, Melbourne 3166, Australia

© Cambridge University Press 1993

First published 1993

Printed in Great Britain at the University Press, Cambridge

A catalogue record for this book is available from the British Library

Library of Congress cataloguing in publication data applied for

ISBN 0 521 44588 4

Project editor: Claire Llewellyn

Cover illustration by Julie Tolliday

Text illustrations by Robina Green, Jackie Morris, Shevanthi de Silva
and Polly Noakes

Contents

Introduction

Poems for more than one voice

When you were very young I'm sure many of you enjoyed saying rhymes together with your parents and at school. Perhaps you still do.

But I expect that most of the poems you enjoy now were written for only one voice. When reading them aloud, you can share them but they were not written with that in mind.

The poems in this book and its companion volume have been written especially for sharing in a pair or group. They are poems with more than one voice, inviting you to take part in a group reading or perhaps a group performance.

They are poems to be read aloud and heard – just like the rhymes you joined in with when you were much younger. I hope you enjoy them.

Enjoying the poems

There are three basic ways of enjoying these poems in a group.

Reading aloud
1 Spend time in a group getting to know the poem by
   - reading it to yourself
   - reading parts aloud together
   - trying different parts to see which combination of voices sounds best
   - sharing your first thoughts about the poem.
2 Decide together how each part should sound. Think about:
   - varying the speed of the reading
   - using pauses
   - varying the sound level, from a whisper to a shout
   - emphasising parts of the poem.
3 Practise reading together the parts for more than one voice.

Talking about the poems

If you want to explore a poem through discussion it might help you to think of questions along these lines:

- What is the poem trying to say?
- How do I feel about the poem?
- What do I particularly like about the poem?
- Has the poem any special meaning for me?
- Are there any parts of the poem not clear to me?
- What do I think about the way it has been written (for example, whether it rhymes or not, its rhythm, its layout, its length, the way it sounds, whether lines and choruses have been repeated, and so on)?

Performing the poems

Because the poems have speaking parts, they are rather like mini-plays which can be performed to an audience. If your group would like to perform some of the poems, you will find some detailed suggestions about how to do this at the back of the book.

The elements reminisce

For four voices

The first two poems in this book take us back to the beginnings of time. They both tell myths, which are stories about the beginning of history. This one is about the creation of Earth.

All   Which of us came first?

Earth   I, when the Creator
scooped me out of darkness,
rolled me in the palm of His hands
and threw me hurtling through space
with a top-spin bowl.

Air   I came next,
when the Creator cupped His hand
to His lips and blew a funnel
of air through space
to curl around you, Earth.

Fire	I came next. Earth was but a frozen ball. From the fire of His belly the Creator drew me forth and breathed me into your dead centre.
Water	I came last. When He shook His head, beads of sweat from His desert-wide brow fanned out into space, some to catch light and fall as stars, others as endless showers of rain.
All	And what does He think of us now?
Earth	He has grown tired of us.
Air	He works in ultra-distant galaxies.
Fire	He is breathing fire into new Earths.
Water	Making each much better than the last until He creates His paradise.
All	But He cannot do without us for He is of us and we of Him.

A creature to sum up Creation

A poem to read around the class

This poem is a myth about how God and the animals planned the creation of the first human family.

1   Over the whole earth
2   flowers teemed
        trees stretched
        shrubs rooted.

1   Over the whole earth
2   lions roared
        elephants pondered
        gazelles sped.

1   Over the whole earth
2   mosquitoes buzzed
        worms burrowed
        ladybirds settled.

1   In the wide sky
2   eagles glided
        doves swarmed
        swallows dipped.

1   In the vast ocean
2   whales sang
        sharks prowled
        salmon leapt.

3   But where was Man
        Woman
        Child?

1, 2 & 3   Unmade.
        There was no Woman, Man, Child
        yet.

3   The God of Creation said

God   I want a creature to sum up Creation.
        You animals, you birds, you insects
        what should Child, Woman, Man be like?

Lion	They should have a roar to make the leaves tremble.
Jaguar	They should have speed to outdistance the wind.
Elephant	They should have strength to shift the mountains.
Monkey	They should have tongues to know how to chatter.
Butterfly	They should have beauty to rival the flowers.
Swallow	They should have wings to give them lightness.
Salmon	They should have gills to swim the great rivers.
Mole	They should have hands to tear the earth.
God	But what should they be like inside themselves?

Gazelle	They should have shyness to know when to hide.
Swan	They should have serenity to know when to drift.
Peacock	They should have vanity to dazzle their thoughts.
Swallow	They should have instinct to guide their journeys.
Tiger	They should have courage to fight their fears.
Tortoise	They should have dreams to fill winter nights.
Lark	They should have song to lift them high.
Dove	They should have hearts to fall in love.
God	All these things I can combine. But what alone beyond all these should I bestow?
All	The spirit, which is your breath.

10

The future

For up to eight voices

In folk tales the sons of the household often have to set off to seek their fortune. In this poem six sons are told to do this by their dying father. He asks them what their plans might be. Their answers are not quite what he expected.

Narrator   Once upon a time . . .
there were six strapping sons.
And what was their crime?
To steal a few blackberries,
to forget about time.
Lately their mother had
quietly died;
each brother had secretly
hidden and cried.
One day their father
called each to his bed.
With shaking beard
he kissed each head.

Father   Boys, I am going
where your mother will be,
across an endless night,
through a deeper sea.
I'm old and I'm weak
and I miss her so.
You too must leave,
all of you, go.
Go out in the world,
discover yourselves
with angels and monsters
and mischievous elves.
So, tell me, my boys
your hopes and your doubts.
But hurry – I feel
my time's running out.

First son   Father, a doctor,
some medicine, please . . .

Father	No, boy, my spirit is lighter than breeze.
Second son	Then do not listen, but rest and sleep.
Father	If I close my eyes I'll be lost in the deep.
Third son	Then we must all talk to keep him alive. We've got to do something to help him survive. Tell what you'll do when you go from here. What do you hope for? What do you fear?
First son	I'll build a castle of crystal glass, our secrets open to all who pass.

Second son	I'll ride horses through the foam of the sea, in the moonlight a-riding, just phantoms and me.
Third son	I'll grow a garden so secret and tall tongues will whisper beyond its great wall.
Fourth son	I'll draw a map of an island unknown where thoughts are reflected in each polished stone.
Fifth son	And I shall plant on the tallest peak our family's motto: "Horizons we seek."
Father	And you, my youngest, where will you go? Nothing, you say, yet your wits are not slow.

Sixth son   I'll keep this house
where our memories are.
Who'll tend your grave
with the family so far?
I'll take my journeys
through the lands of the mind,
no shortage of wonders or
treasures I'll find.
So father, be sure,
we'll discover ourselves,
with angels and monsters
and mischievous elves.

Narrator   With that the old man
closed his dimming eyes.
Who told the truth?
Who told the lies?
Tired though he was,
he pondered this deep,
into the darkness,
the dark beyond sleep.

13

Whisked away

For four voices

This is a science-fiction poem. It describes a village devastated – by what? Only a few clues are given.

1 Once there was a village,
2 an empty village,
3 an eerily empty village,
4 and in that village
1 there was a street,
2 a littered street,
3 a windswept littered street,
4 and in that street
1 there was a house,
2 an echoing house,
3 an innocent echoing house,
4 and in that house
1 there was a door,
2 an open door,
3 a creaking open door,
4 and in that door
1 there was a lock,
2 a smashed lock,
3 a brutally smashed lock.
4 And through that door
1 there was a hall,
2 a dusty hall,
3 a dusty leaf-strewn hall,
4 and in that hall
1 there were some stairs,
2 some cobwebbed stairs,
3 stairs with no footprints
All *save those of the wild cats.*

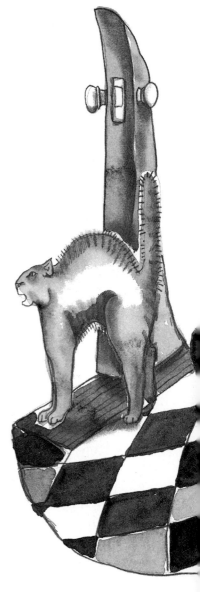

4 At the top of these stairs
1 there was a room,
2 a child's room,
3 a lost child's room,
4 and in that room
1 there was a desk,
2 a little desk,
3 a little child's desk,
4 and on that desk
1 there was a tape recorder
2 with a tape still inside
3 wound to its end.

All *Who will play that tape?*
Who is there now who will listen
to the story it tells?

4 And on that tape
1 there was a sound,
2 a heavy sound,
3 the sound of a voice crying

All *"Help, help, help . . ."*

4 And beside that sound
1 was another sound
2 of footsteps,
3 heavy footsteps

All *coming slowly up the stairs*
up the stairs, slowly . . .

4 And near the tape
1 was a writing pad
2 on which had been scrawled
3 the lost child's name,
4 and beside that name
1 was a print,
2 a paw-print,
3 the print of a paw never seen on Earth

All *like a signature.*
4 It was the only sign of what happened
1 to the village,
2 the empty village
3 the eerily empty village

All *where the wild cats played.*

Pink flamingos

For three voices

This poem is really a fable, and like most fables it has a message in it somewhere. What is that message? That's for you to find out – if you want to. If you're not bothered about the message, just enjoy the poem as a rather unusual story.

1   This is the story of a smallish girl

2   a smallish girl who went to an airport

3   to an airport and boarded the wrong plane.

1   She boarded a silver plane
painted with pink flamingos.

2   Pink flamingos: how could a smallish girl

3   with nutbrown eyes and the energy of a bird

2   how could this smallish girl
resist such an aeroplane?

1   The pink flamingos took her,
took her through clouds into a strange land,

2   a dreamy sort of land
where all the people, everyone, stood

3   stood on one leg, yes, everyone
stood on one leg,

1   and all were silent. All you could hear
was the quiet brush brush of little paint brushes

2   brush brush on large canvases

3   tall canvases, for they did little but
paint paint paint all day long:

1   people painting

2   and standing

3   on one leg

All   all day long.

1   The smallish girl watched birdlike
with her nutbrown eyes, watched and waited

2   and gathered all the pictures she liked best
given by the painters who liked her smile.

3 She took them home and gazed at them,
      gazed lovingly, letting them enter her dreams.

1 But one day, not being able to live on dreams,
      she took the pictures to an art gallery

2 a very important art gallery
      and there they caused a huge sensation.

All WHAT A SENSATION!

1 And so she sold them all, and counted her money,
      counted cascades of money in her bare home.

2 At night, in her bare home, her dreams faded
      until there was only darkness

3 darkness and the endless echo
      echo of the brush brush, brush brush

1 of the one-legged painters far away.

2 So she went back to the airport,
      back to find the pink flamingo plane,

3 and there it was on the runway
      like a giant flamingo

1 a giant flamingo poised to take flight.

2 But in her excitement, a desperate excitement
      to visit once more that strange land

3 the land where everyone stood

1 stood on one leg

2 and painted, painted, painted all day long,

3 she caught the wrong plane, yes, the wrong one,

1 and landed in a country, an ordinary country
      teeming with tourists

2 tourists resolutely on two legs

3 none of whom could paint

1 and only a few of whom
      could stand on one leg for any length of time,

2 none of whom resembled a flamingo.

3 This is the story of a smallish girl
      a smallish girl who went to an airport

1 and another

2 and another

3 and another

1 searching for painted pink flamingos

2 searching

3 and searching

1 and searching

2 but finding nothing but flags and emblems,
flags, emblems and tourists,

3 searching for the aeroplane
the pink flamingo aeroplane
that lived like a dream in her eyes.

Aunt and Uncle's travels

For four voices

Why do people go on long, hazardous treks in faraway places? Is it just to see unusual sights? Or are they searching for something else?

Aunt We've travelled the land of perpetual ice
    where moonlight is winter's day,
and the creeping glacier is all you can see
    except where the penguins play.

Uncle We've trekked through the dust of hot desert sand
    where the sunlight peels your eyes,
and the waving mirage is all you can see
    in a world of hazy lies.

Aunt We've hacked through forests of steamy light
    where rain sheets down in a hiss,
and the rainbow's crazy over the trees
    where monkeys shriek their bliss . . .

Nephew But do tell us, Uncle,
do tell us this:
why do you travel so wide?

Niece You could have dreamt
such traveller's tales
here by your fireside.

Uncle We travelled the land of perpetual ice
    for the Yeti, the abominable one . . .

Aunt but on hearing the note of its eerie cry
    we froze; and then it was gone.

Uncle We trekked through the dust of hot desert sand
    to be part of a shimmering mirage . . .

Aunt but all is scrub and dunes out there
    with its taunting camouflage.

Uncle We hacked through forests of steamy light
    in search of the rainbow's end . . .

Aunt but the crock of gold we should have found
was drowned in the river's bend.

Nephew But do tell us, Aunt,
do tell us this:
why did you search for a dream?

Niece You could have sat
by your cottage fire,
watching the firelight gleam.

Aunt We travelled the land for a legend.
We trekked the sand for a dream.

Uncle We looked for gold at the end of light:
this is our life-long theme.

One Christmas Eve

For six voices

One snowy Christmas Eve a child opens the door and sees
ghostlike figures from the Christmas story. Why have they come?
Why do they look so faint and transparent? Is it all a dream?

Child   I opened the door
upon a snowy hill.
There stood a sheep
like a phantom, so still.
"Where have you come from,
my little sheep,
when all of your kind
are huddled in sleep?"

Sheep   I have seen stars
that from the sky
turned into angels,
made men cry.
I have heard voices
that sang of a king,
the hills ablaze
with the light of their wings.

Child   What is that wavering
like a strange ghost,
there – a pale man –
by the shadowy post?

Shepherd   I was a shepherd
on that singing night
when we were all summoned
to a birth of light.
Confused, we all were,
to leave our sheep,
but we had a journey,
a promise to keep.

Child   And is that behind you,
nodding its head,
a ghost of a donkey
with silent tread?

22

Donkey I was a part
of that holy day,
so thankful to munch
the innkeeper's hay;
so shaken, too,
when I heard that cry,
shaken, then stilled
by the mother's sigh.

Sheep I followed on
where the shepherd led,
walking through streets
without any dread . . .

Shepherd All of us bathed
in the unnatural light
that haloed the head
of the babe that night.

Star   And I shone down
from mysteries afar,
guiding three camels
by the glint of my star,
pulled through the night
on invisible thread
to lead three kings
to an infant's bed.

Camel   I was confused
when we came to a king
whose soft-sounding words
had a snakelike sting.
But then, travelling on,
my masters soon found
where to lay presents
on hallowed ground.

Shepherd	Animals and angels,
	poor shepherds too,
	a king in the hay,
	a star in the blue;
	thus did we stand
	and wonder why
	God sent this infant
	down from on high.
Child	Why do you come now,
	why to me,
	haunting this hillside
	by the sea?
	Long since those days
	have passed us by;
	we remember that eve
	if we but try;
	Bethlehem's gone,
	you've strayed so far,
	Sheep and Shepherd,
	Camel and Star.
All but the Child	It's ours to wander
	through other's sleep,
	to raise our story
	from the deep.
	Touched by that light
	we try to keep
	vigil for each child
	lost in sleep.
Child	But now you are fading –
	why do you go?
	Fainter than shadows,
	colder than snow.
	Thank you for coming
	this Christmas Eve;
	that you were all here
	I'll try and believe . . .
	Empty the night now,
	empty the hill;
	was there anything there
	in the starry chill?

The seasons' marathon

For four voices

Have you ever heard of a race that lasts a whole year?

Spring S o here we stand again
P oised at the starting line,
R *eady* . . .
I nching out of our winter's rest. *Steady* . . .
N ew in our green sportswear. So, it's –
G *o*, down the track of the year.

Summer S ome of us jockey for space,
U nhurried clematis moving up fast while bluebells
and daffodils trail.
M anic man disqualifies left and right,
M anaging the rest with no sort of fairness:
E lder gets held back while
R hubarb streaks ahead.

Autumn A show of fatigue is not noticeable
U ntil the frailer ones fall.
T he track is littered with sun-stroked bodies
U rged across the line of death.
M an gathers our trophies: the golden apples,
N uts for their winter gloating.

Winter W e all brood –
I n the long freeze – brood that while
N ature fires the pistol, lays the track,
T ime has tamed us all;
E ach winter telling us it's the journey, not the
R ace that counts.

Hey, little pond skater

For three voices

I was watching a pond skater resting on the surface of a friend's garden pond. Beneath the insect were some large, shadowy fish. It occurred to me how dark and confined the lives of those fish were in comparison to the pond skater. It can peer down into the dark world of the pond from the light and freedom of its own.

Pike
Hey, little pond skater,
    what do you see,
skimming in the shadows
    of a mirrored tree?
What's it like in the sun
    where the green frog croaks?
What keeps you alive
    in the air that chokes?

Pond skater
My world is a mirror
of moody light,
a dish of stars
in a cold, clear night.
I skate past lilies
and skim past reeds,
pause where reflections
wave in weeds.

Carp
Hey, little pond skater,
    who gave you feet
to balance on the line
    where our two worlds meet?
Why do you tease us
    through summer's quarter,
dodging our jaws
    as you skate the water?

Pond skater
I rest on the thinnest
film of light.
To peer in the dark
is a strange delight.
There you drift

like forgotten thoughts,
the O of your mouths,
the bubbling noughts.

Pike   Hey, little pond skater,
        where do you go
when you're tired of our water;
        how can we know?
Tell us of birds
        and tell us of bees,
tell of the wind that
        sings in the trees.

Pond   These things that you speak of
skater are not for your eyes;
besides, you would think them
a queer pack of lies.
Just as I try not
to enter your gloom,
stick to your own world;
up here there's no room.

Carp Hey, little pond skater,
        you're not being fair.
     We're stuck in this dark;
        you can fly anywhere.
     Come a bit closer,
        tell all you know,
     for you will be dead
        come the first winter snow.

Pond My world is a mirror
skater of moody light,
     a dish of stars
     in a cold, clear night.
     When fins become legs
     and you grow wings,
     then, only then,
     will you know of these things.

Pike and Hey, little pond skater,
Carp   what do you see,
     skimming in the shadows
        of a mirrored tree?
     We'll keep on asking
        each time you appear.
     Perhaps you'll answer
        when winter draws near.

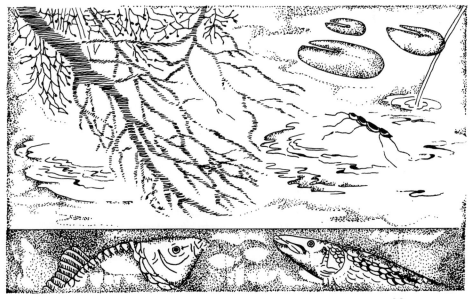

What the trees say

For five voices

Writers of stories and poems often ask themselves "What if . . .?"
In this poem I ask, "What if trees could communicate with each
other? What would they say?"

Willow Think of the rain dancing
a tattoo upon our dripping leaves,
watery sprites kicking up their
transparent heels.

Elm Think of the sleek badger
who lately came among us,
a night visitor
snuffling secrets in our roots.

Oak I'd rather think of the
baying sweep of hounds,
of the trembling fox
emerging unscathed from the leaves.

Beech I shall think of a quieter time
in spring when the schoolboy
leant against me and tested the air
with a song to startle the birds.

Wind *Remember, I can sweep through you all,*
Teach you a lesson in Nature's hard school.
Tear off your branches,
Tear out your roots,
I, the wind, a devil when it suits.

Willow Think of the snow folding
white about our nakedness,
swathing us ghostlike
as if for a silent wedding.

Oak I shall think more fondly
of the girls who sat in our arms
and weaved such nonsense about our leaves;
we all listened to that.

Elm But what of that distant intermittent
whine of a giant bee we hear,
the way we sense an untimely death?
Do you not shiver?

Beech We are safe here: think of the woman
who wanders among us like a green spirit,
tending our saplings like a nurse.
Don't you smile when she hums to us?

Wind *Remember, I can sweep through you all,*
Teach you a lesson in Nature's hard school.
Tear off your branches,
Tear out your roots,
I, the wind, a devil when it suits.

Headlines of a very ordinary day

For three voices or for reading around in class

If you read the "popular press" (the smaller-sized newspapers) you may have noticed that they use words in a special way. Their headlines try to catch your attention, often exaggerating the events being reported. This poem plays with the language of headlines as it reports an ordinary school day in the life of Joseph, aged about ten.

One winter morning Joseph closed his garden gate
and trudged off through the snow to school.

BOY EXPLORER LOST IN ARCTIC BLIZZARDS
School authorities in uproar

He rolled a snowball and threw it at the sky.

MYSTERY MISSILE CRASH LANDS FROM OUTER SPACE
Scientists fly in from around the world

He greeted his friend Jonathan.

BRILLIANT LINGUISTS CRACK NEW LANGUAGE CODE

They went into school to start their maths.

CHILD PRODIGIES SOLVE WORLD'S MOST COMPLEX EQUATION

Later they worked on a poem.

POEM STUNS WORLD CONFERENCE
I give up, says Poet Laureate

They finished writing a story.

CHILD WRITERS A CERT FOR BOOKER PRIZE
Top authors complain

At break they resumed a football match.

TOP SELECTORS FIGHT OVER STARS IN CRUCIAL REPLAY

After that, they went in to paint a picture in the style of Van Gogh.

BRILLIANT FORGERS REVEAL SECRETS OF THEIR ART
Critics overwhelmed with shame

At lunch Joseph had a salad
and Jonathan had a beefburger.

VEGETARIANS FIGHT MEAT LOBBY
Many injured in school row

As it was cold outside, they stayed in to play chess.

GRAND MASTERS THROW IN THE TOWEL
What's the use? says top Russian player

In the afternoon they worked on electricity and magnetism in science.

SPECTACULAR LIGHT SHOW PRAISED BY PM AT LOCAL SCHOOL
TV audiences dazzled

To finish the school day the teacher rehearsed the class for tomorrow's assembly.

WHOLE NEW ERA IN ACTING, SAY STUNNED CRITICS

On the way home they peered into an amusement arcade.

GAMBLING JUNKIES IN UNDER-AGE SWOOP

They stopped to buy some chips.

OVER-WEIGHT PUPILS ON KILLER DIETS

At the street corner Joseph said goodbye to Jonathan.

SECRET OF BLOOD BROTHERS' TERRIBLE SPLIT

He trudged back home and opened the garden gate.

MIRACULOUS SURVIVAL OF BLIZZARD BOY
It's amazing he's alive, say doctors

His mum called, "You're late. Where've you been?"

ECSTASY OF FRANTIC MOTHER
Nothing could make me happier now that my long-lost boy is home again, says mother at centre of the blizzard boy row

Later Joseph watched television.

TV BRAINWASHES NATION'S YOUTH
Headteachers complain at special conference

He did some history homework.

I WAS CAESAR'S SOOTHSAYER, CLAIMS HISTORY FREAK

And then he went to bed.

BLIZZARD BOY IN DEEP COMA
Will he ever wake up? cries worried mother.

The dinner report

For reading around in a group

The weather report on the television is not the most exciting of programmes, is it? In this poem I have used the language of weather reports to describe a rather noisy, argumentative family. Could you do the same with your family?

At the dinner table tonight
we expect a swirl of tight isobars
centring just above the Lancashire Hotpot.

Over Mother we think there'll be
a sudden squall and a sharp rain of words;

but further south, round the Isle of Dad,
there could be the odd burst of sunshine
in amongst the threatening clouds.

In the Infant Lowlands we expect
persistent dampness and the odd howling gale;

further up, in the Granny Highlands
there's almost certain to be a sharp frost.

Towards the Adolescent South-West
the fog will persist overnight
and be somewhat hazardous by morning.

In fact, the best weather is likely to be
in the Little Sister region
where warm air from a calm and cloudless night
has already reached the coast.

What shall we do with Jason?

For three voices

Sadness often makes people want to withdraw; to be on their
own, while they try and cope with their feelings. This behaviour
is sometimes difficult for their friends to understand.

Michael   What shall we do with Jason?
He won't come out to play.

Sally   It's nothing but the telly
since his grandad went away.

Michael   Where'd his grandad go to?
Jason wouldn't tell.

Mum   His mum thinks he's in heaven.
And his step-dad says – in hell.

Sally   So Jason's grandad died, then?
That's bad. We didn't know.

Mum   They were very close, I'd say,
as close as these things go.
His mum was forced to work, you see,
when Jason was a tot.
His grandad wheeled him down the street
and rocked him in his cot.

Michael   But what about the father, then?
Our Jason's never told us.

Mum   Some things you never do find out.
Some things are left mysterious.

Sally   What shall we do with Jason, then?
He won't come out to play.

Michael   Just scowls at us when we go round
since his grandad went away.

Mum   Why not hold a party
and insist he come along?
Ignore his scowls and shyness,
pretend there's nothing wrong.
Form a village football team

or cricket if you like.
Think about a picnic
to the seaside, or a hike.

Sally   What shall we do with Jason?
He doesn't want these things.

Michael   He just walked by us yesterday
when we called him from the swings.

Sally   His face has changed, it's gone all white
and long, as if he's cried.

Michael   We've called, we're kind, he won't join in.
Can't say we haven't tried.

Sally   What shall we do with Jason?
To us he's still a friend.

Mum   Just be there when his sadness
comes to an end.

Give us a job

For four voices

If you know someone who's been looking for a job for a long time, you'll know how desperate they can become. "I'll try anything," you may have heard them say. Anything? There are some strange jobs about. What about the ones being advertised in this poem? This is a sideways look at a serious problem.

All   Give us a job,
give us a job,
we're part of the mob
without a job.
We're Carol and John
and Tina and Bob,
out there searching,
give us a job.

1   Wanted: a clown to stand on his head,
to keep me company when I'm in bed.
Must be keen and sing like a bird,
be able to mime and not say a word.

All   That's not for us. So
give us a job . . .
(*repeat the chorus*)

2   Wanted: a pair to explore Outer Space
(must be desperate to quit this place).
Out in the stars on a mystery track –
Exciting! Stupendous! (But you may not come back.)

All   That's not for us. So
give us a job . . .
(*repeat the chorus*)

3   Wanted: someone to tutor a charming child,
manners not perfect, perhaps a bit wild.
Suit someone nicely who's worked in a zoo
with chimpanzees, monkeys: could that be you?

All   That's not for us. So
give us a job . . .
(*repeat the chorus*)

4 Wanted: a person with nerves of steel
   to chase away ghosts. (Well, of course they're real.)
   For centuries they've haunted my stately home,
   made all my guests gibber, tremble and foam.

All That's not for us. So
     give us a job
     give us a job,
     we're part of the mob
     without a job.
     We're Carol and John
     and Tina and Bob,
     we're looking for something,
     not any old job.
     Would you apply for
     one of these posts?
     You'd have to be jester
     and angel and ghost.
     Give us a job,
     not any old job,
     we're Carol and John
     and Tina and Bob.

Traveller's child

For seven voices

This is a poem which gives six different views of the same
person, a schoolgirl called Annabel. She lives in a caravan with
her father who works on the roads. As he has to move from job
to job, so she has to move from school to school. Each verse
gives clues about the children who are speaking their thoughts
about her.

Sharon   Do I like her? I like the way
her dark plaits flow down the back of her hair,
and she seems proud of her funny clothes.
She doesn't say much, but we all know
what she wants: I envy that. She says
she's got a stack of *My Guy* I can read
but looks disgusted when I mention boys.
She's been to my home twice now,
acted a bit strange I thought, awkward.
Mum says she has cat-like eyes.
There's a mystery about where she lives:
I wonder why? And do I like her?

Susan   This is my chance, I thought,
to find a real friend at last,
not those who are nice to you on your own
and then nasty to you in a group;
someone I can tell my burning secret to.
I sit at her table,
I lend her my swimming cap,
I pick her first in games,
I warn her against certain boys.
But she never really notices me.
Those green eyes just stare right through me.
Why? What have I done wrong?

Sandra   Look at her, the way she swaggers in class
as if she owns the place. One of these days
I'll tie those little-girl plaits into a
knot so hard she'll never undo it.
She thinks she's so cool and clever,
smarming up to the teacher. Yet,

you never hear where she lives,
where she comes from with her funny accent.
There's something fishy here:
I'll find out what it is,
then we'll see who runs this class.

Darren   Suddenly, there she is, tall, beautiful,
right in the centre of my daydreams
in that leather waistcoat and multicoloured socks.
We lock arms and roam the streets, heads together –
a dazzling couple.
And I think of nothing but her, her, her:
her name is written on everything I touch.
Yet never will I have the courage to tell her,
never: she makes me feel so foolish
when she looks at me.

Ian   Who'd believe that behind that smile's a spitting cat?
I followed her out of the school gates
and across the allotments to the little lane.
"Why are you following me, Bolan?"
I turned on the charm. "I like the way you walk,
the way your plaits swing, your nice legs . . ."
I thought she'd knock me over.
If anyone had seen what she did
I'd have died a thousand shames.
Mum guessed when she saw the flaming patch on my
cheek.
It burns inside me.
I'd better steer clear of that girl.

Annabel   Dear Mum, this school's not too bad
though there's some funny kids in my class.
There's one that's really jealous of me,
and another keeps pestering me to take her home –
but how can I let her know how I live?
That's when I wish I'd stayed with you.
Then there's a girl I feel sorry for,
she's cold-shouldered by the rest
because she tries too hard to be friends.
I have boy trouble too – when didn't I?
Some of them stare at me as if moonstruck;
one got a beautiful slap on the cheek.
Dad's moving on soon, he says; it's a pity,

I'll never make friends at this rate.
I'm so lonely. I'll write again soon.

Teacher   We are all sorry that Annabel is leaving so soon.
She was very popular with the other children.
Her cleverness was well hidden and perhaps
she was a little too quiet for her own good,
but I know that we will all miss her.

Jack-a-penny

For three voices

This is a poem that insisted on being written. One morning I
wrote two poems and I thought, that's enough for one day. But
all afternoon I felt there was another poem inside me waiting to
come out. This is a curious, unsettling feeling. Suddenly, at
about four o'clock (yes, I even remember the time), the first line
came into my head, followed almost at once by the second. The
rest of the poem seemed to write itself. On re-reading the poem,
there were only a handful of lines to be changed – and it was
finished.

**First
woman**

Jack-a-penny, lack-a-penny,
mud upon your boots,
have you been a-grubbing
in the wood's dark roots?
What d'you hope to find there,
buried what and why?
Jack-a-penny, lack-a-penny,
tell us now, don't lie.

**Second
woman**

Jack-a-penny, lack-a-penny,
mud upon your boots,
do you share a secret
with the worms and the newts?
Everyday you search there,
buried what and why?
Jack-a-penny, lack-a-penny,
tell us now, don't lie.

Tramp

*I'm Jack-a-penny, lack-a-penny,
in my dreams I see
the child as I was
in the roots of a tree.
All my life I've lived here,
shadowed in this wood,
I'm looking now for what I've lost
to make me good.*

First woman	Jack-a-penny, lack-a-penny, mud upon your boots, what is it that you have lost down among the roots? Can you hope to find it all these years gone by? Jack-a-penny, lack-a-penny, Tell us now, don't lie.
Tramp	*"Jack-a-penny, lack-a-penny," my mother said to me, "Go take this sovereign, hide it 'neath a tree; lest your father find it, lest the robbers roam, for there's nothing safe but hunger in our poor, wee home."*

44

Second woman	Jack-a-penny, lack-a-penny, mud upon your boots, where d'you put that sovereign in the wood's dark roots? You could search all day and night, search the whole year through. Jack-a-penny, lack-a-penny, come on home, do.
Tramp	*I'm Jack-a-penny, lack-a-penny, nothing but my name; hunger in my belly and half-blind, lame. Nothing else for me to do, with mud upon my boots, than to search for that sovereign in the wood's dark roots . . .*
	to search for that sovereign in the wood's dark roots.

Granny and child

For two voices

There is a mystery in this poem. Is there something a little strange about Granny?

Granny, Granny, do come quick!
What is it, child?
I feel rather sick.
You look rather wild.

I saw something out there.
But it's dark, no light . . .
A figure. A shadow.
You imagined it, right?

No, Granny, no, it was there,
down by the garden shed.
Well, there's nothing there now.
Why don't you go back to bed?

I'm frightened, Granny.
It stood there so still.
If you go on like this, child,
you'll make yourself ill.

It wore a tall hat, Granny,
and a long black shawl.
You must try to sleep, child,
tomorrow, it's school.

But I saw it there, Granny,
looking this way.
Hush, child, forget it.
Do as I say.

Yes, all right, Granny,
but you'll leave on the light?
Oh, you're much too big
to be afraid of the night.

It was waiting to snatch me,
of that I felt sure.
Oh, Granny, please Granny,
you will bolt the door?

This is all a bad dream, child.
But if you like I will say
a nice little spell
to dissolve it away.

A spell, Granny? You?
But you're not a witch . . .
Don't be silly, my girl.
Now, my hand's on the switch.

But you'll leave on the light?
And you will bolt the door?
You're quite safe, my child.
Do forget what you saw.

Haven't you got a shawl, Granny,
just like that?
And in the dressing-up box
there's a tall black hat . . .

Oh, you'll have bad dreams
if you think like that.
Now sleep, my girl,
or you'll make me wild.

Goodnight, then, Granny.
Goodnight, my child.

Nightmare

For two voices

This is a disturbing poem. Is it about a nightmare? Or is it about something that is really happening?

1   Sit alone upon a chair.
2   Twist in finger lock of hair.
1   No one with you. No one there.
2   Twist in finger lock of hair.

1   Listen for a heavy step.
    Listen for a creaking stair.
2   No one with you. No one there.
    Twist in finger lock of hair.

1   Hear door opening, hear door close.
    Listen for the creaking stair.
2   No one with you. No one there.
    Twist in finger lock of hair.

1   Soft the light from open door,
    shadow on the breathing floor.
2   No one with you.
1   *Someone there.*
2   No one with you.
1   *Who will care?*

Performing the poems

Reading a poem aloud is one thing. Acting it is quite another. When you act a poem you must know the words by heart and have prepared suitable actions, perhaps even sound effects, to go with them. Acting a poem is like putting on a mini-play for your audience.

If you would like to perform some of these poems, you may find the following advice useful. Discuss the points in your group and with your teacher. Specific suggestions for individual poems are on pages 51–56.

General points

1 Who will be your audience? Have you chosen a poem you think they will like and understand?
2 Are you really interested in the poem yourself? Is it one you want to spend time on? Is it one you want to learn by heart and share with others?
3 Do you feel comfortable working with the people in your group?
4 Do you all understand the poem you have chosen? If not, talk about what puzzles you. You can often understand a poem better by sharing what you think about it with others.
5 Between you, choose the parts of the poem you are going to perform carefully. Is your voice the most suitable one for your part?
6 Together, read the poem aloud several times. Talk about how each part might sound. Ask yourselves these questions:
   • Are there parts which need to be faster or slower than others?
   • Do some parts need to be louder or quieter than others?
   • Are there any parts or sounds which need emphasising?
   • Would sound effects help?
7 Next, as a group, copy the poem into the middle of a large sheet of paper. Make notes around the poem to remind yourselves what was agreed. You can

underline certain words or highlight them. This will be your working script.

8 Practise reading the poem into a tape recorder. Play it back and discuss how it might be improved.

9 Parts of some of the poems are spoken by two or more voices together. These are usually marked **All** which refers to all those who have parts in the poem. Sometimes, however, parts for more than one voice are printed in italics and this allows for other people, who may not have a part, to join in. This is usually called a chorus. Practise the chorus carefully so that everyone knows exactly how to say it and the words remain clear.

10 Now learn your part of the poem by heart. When you perform your poem you won't be *reading* it, you will be *performing* it. There is a big difference. Your performance will be more like something acted on the radio than read from a page.

11 Next, rehearse your "mini-play" together. Tape it again, and listen to how it sounds. Do you need to make any final changes? You could ask one or two friends what they think of it.

12 At this point you will need to decide whether any mime, movement or acting would help make the poem more enjoyable for the audience. If you do not want to do this yourself, another group might be willing to mime actions while you perform the poem.

13 Only perform your poem when you all feel confident. It will help the audience if one of you introduces the poem, saying where it is set and what it is about.

This preparation is likely to take quite a time, especially if the poem is a long one. It can't always be done in one session. You may well not have enough class time for it, so think about getting together at lunchtime, after school or at weekends.

Suggestions for individual poems

The elements reminisce

1 Make sure your audience know what the four elements are – earth, air, fire and water. One way to make this clear is to have four chairs facing the audience, each labelled with the name of one of the elements. You stand in a group to one side, then take your seat one by one before starting the poem.

2 To create the right mood for this piece, you could play part of a suite of music called *The Planets* by the composer Gustav Holst before and after the performance, or even as a quiet background throughout the performance, if you find that this works in rehearsals.

3 You could link the performance to the next poem: "A creature to sum up Creation".

A creature to sum up Creation

1 This is a poem that the whole class could perform. The first three speakers should stand at the front. The person playing God should be with them, centre stage.

The future

1 The poem is a deathbed scene. The person playing the father should be lying under a cover as if he is in bed, weak and dying. His six sons should be sitting around him.

2 The Narrator should stand to one side, addressing the audience.

3 The father should sound very old. When each son says what he is going to do with his life, he should kneel by his father and speak directly to him.

Whisked away

1 A picture and some props may help make the performance of this poem more effective. On one side display a large picture of what is described in the first part of the poem: an open door with a smashed lock, a leaf-strewn hall, cobwebbed stairs,

wild cats. On the other side have a desk on which there is a tape recorder, a writing pad with a name on it and a large paw-print. On the tape should be the voice of a child crying for help and the sound of heavy footsteps: play this at the appropriate moment.

2 When you have finished the performance, ask your audience what they think could have happened to the village.

Pink flamingos

This story needs to be told directly to the audience with no actions or props. You are three storytellers sharing the same story. Sit in a row and speak to your audience as if you are letting them into a strange secret.

Aunt and Uncle's travels

1 Aunt and Uncle should be seated centre stage: they are the storytellers. The niece and nephew could be on either side of them, or perhaps sitting at their feet.

2 There is nothing ordinary about Aunt and Uncle – they are inspired, trying to make lifelong dreams come true. You somehow have to convey this to your audience. Gestures will help, but it is the tone of voice you use which will have the most effect.

3 The niece and nephew are a little puzzled. Do they nod their heads in understanding at the end of the poem?

One Christmas Eve

1 This poem is like a short play and is, of course, best performed at Christmas.

2 Decide how you are going to make clear to the audience what parts you are playing. Will you use masks for the sheep, donkey, star and camel, with a costume and crook for the shepherd, or will you simply wear large badges saying who you are?

3 Think about where you position yourself. The Child should stand apart; the other performers should make a tableau, moving only when they speak.

4 At the end of the poem, everyone but the child could slowly leave the stage so that it's empty by the end of the verse.

The seasons' marathon

There are two ways you could perform this poem, simply or more elaborately with mime.

1 The simple way: stand in a row facing your audience. Make sure it is clear who each of you represents. As Spring and Summer say their verses, all of you jog on the spot as if running in a race. Slow down as Autumn begins and by the end of Autumn's verse you should have fallen down. For Winter's verse sit in a circle.

2 The elaborate way: space yourselves out, facing the audience. Behind or beside each speaker is a small group of classmates who act out what is happening in each verse as it is spoken. This will need careful rehearsing. All of the speakers say *Ready . . . Steady . . . Go.*

Hey, little pond skater

1 For this, try making large, two-dimensional stick puppets of the pike, the carp and the pond skater (using information books to get the details accurate). These should then "speak" the poem. The pond skater on top of the water should, of course, be held higher than the fish.

2 You could also experiment with voice effects for the fish, perhaps speaking down a tube to create a deep, slightly muffled effect – but make sure the result is not a funny one.

What the trees say

1 Explain to the audience that four of you are trees in a wood and that one of you is the wind.

2 The wind should weave in and out among the trees, addressing each one with its menacing words.

Headlines of a very ordinary day

1 For this poem you need a narrator, two boys acting the parts of Joseph and Jonathan, and at least two people to shout the headlines.
2 The headlines could be painted in black on large sheets of white paper and held up as they are shouted.
3 Allow long enough pauses between the lines for the two boys to mime the different actions in the day.

The dinner report

1 With your teacher's help, photocopy onto an overhead projector transparency an outline of the British Isles, with few or no place names marked. Write on it, labelling places for Mother, Isle of Dad, Infant Lowlands, Granny Highlands, Adolescent South-West and the Little Sister region. Using an overhead projector, project the image onto a wall or pinboard where your audience can see it clearly.
2 Make symbols or signs on card for rain, cloud, sun, frost, fog and warm temperatures. These are to be fixed to the projected map either before or while the poem is spoken – try this beforehand to see which method works best. Isobars can be drawn over Mother and the Infant Lowlands.
3 Decide how many speakers the poem will have and practise it. Try to copy the tone of voice used by real weather reporters on the television.

What shall we do with Jason?

Two of Jason's friends are discussing him with their mother. The three speakers could be sitting around a meal table as they talk.

Give us a job

1 The four advertisements in this poem should be written on postcards and pinned on a noticeboard with the sign "Small Ads". They are then "read aloud" by the speakers.
2 The chorus can be chanted as the four of you tramp around, moving in a circle from and back to the

noticeboard. The last chorus could be said as a direct appeal to the audience.

Traveller's child

1 Each person in this poem is speaking their thoughts aloud. No one else can hear them.
2 Annabel should be sitting on her own at a desk, writing the letter to her mum. As she writes, the speakers come in one at a time and stand looking at her as they say their verse; they then step aside. Annabel goes on writing, unaware of the speakers. Finally, she reads aloud her letter, gets up and leaves. The teacher then comes on to round off the poem.

Jack-a-penny

1 Explain to the audience that the poem takes place in a wood. Simple costumes for the tramp and two women might also be useful.
2 Jack should be searching for something – but slowly, as if without much hope of success – before the women appear and begin to speak. He should speak slowly, too, as befits a weary old man. The women are sympathetic but worried about him. His last verse should show signs of irritation and desperation; you can't help feeling sorry for him.

Granny and child

1 The girl in the poem should begin by looking out of the window. She sees something frightening, stares, and calls out for her granny.
2 Granny should be played in such a way that the audience is left with the doubt that she might not be all that she seems. Is she being sympathetic or is she trying to hide something from her grandchild?

Nightmare

1 This is a serious poem and should not be turned into a horror story. Try to leave disturbing questions about the child in the audience's mind. There should be no sound effects.
2 The first speaker should sit on a chair facing the audience, nervously twisting a finger in a lock of

hair. Every time the word "listen" is said, he or she should stop, stiffen and listen, while the audience wonders whether the sounds are real or imagined. During the last verse, the speaker could rise from the chair, and walk off backwards as if something menacing had entered the room.

3 The two speakers must make careful use of tone, pauses and pace to create the maximum effect.